LEAD *the* LIGHT WAY™

LEADERSHIP TRAINING FOR CHURCH MEMBERS

by Beverly K. Girton

Published by:

Leading the LIGHT Way HR, LLC

Fort Worth, Texas

ISBN: 979-8-9931687-0-8

Printed in the United States of America

DISCLAIMER

This book is a work of teaching, reflection, and inspiration. It is intended for educational and ministry development purposes only. It is **not legal, psychological, or professional counseling advice**. Readers should seek guidance from qualified professionals for personal, organizational, or legal concerns.

DEDICATION

To my husband, **John E. Girton, III**, whose constant prayers and words of encouragement have been a steady light in my life. I thank God for John's Light, Love, and Leadership.

To my sister, **Lilisa J. Williams (CoachLilisa)**, my forerunner in this work. You helped pull this out of me when you invited me to present at a leadership conference. Thank you for helping me "Release my Power."

ACKNOWLEDGMENTS

This work is the result of many prayers, conversations, and encouragement from those who believe in the LIGHT principles of **Love, Integrity, Goodness, Humility, and Transparency**.

I give glory to God for the wisdom and guidance He has given me to bring this training to life. To every church leader, volunteer, co-worker, mentor, and friend who has shared their experiences and trusted me to walk alongside them thank you.

A special thanks to the many leaders who opened up about their struggles and joys in leadership. Your honesty has shaped these pages more than you know.

Most of all, I acknowledge the Lord Jesus Christ, the true Light of the world (John 8:12). Without Him, there is no leadership worth following.

Table of Contents

CHAPTER 1

Introduction: Lighting the Path, Lightening the
Load

Leadership is often described as influence, vision, or strategy. But for those who have carried the real weight of it, leadership is also a burden. It requires decisions that affect people's lives, conversations that carry consequences, and responsibilities that can feel never ending. Many leaders find themselves awake at night, replaying situations in their mind, wondering if they said or did the right thing.

The **LIGHT Way** offers something different. It is a way of leading that not only **lights the path for others** but also **lightens the load for the leader**. Instead of carrying leadership as a constant strain, the LIGHT principles create peace, clarity, and direction.

These five principles **Love, Integrity, Goodness, Humility, and Transparency** are like windows that allow light to shine through. When the windows are clear, the light flows freely, illuminating the path for everyone. When they are clouded with fear, pride, or compromise, leadership becomes heavy, confusing, and ineffective.

Why LIGHT Leadership Matters

The world is full of leadership models, from corporate strategies to ministry training programs. But too often, those models focus on results without considering the people carrying out the mission. A church can grow quickly but leave its volunteers burned out. A business can hit its profit goals but damage its people in the process. A leader can look successful from the outside but feel empty and exhausted within.

LIGHT Leadership is different because it is **people centered and mission driven**. It's not about being perfect, it's about being aligned. When your values, words, and actions are aligned with the LIGHT principles, you create an environment where both the mission and the people can thrive.

The Balance of the Five Principles

One of the most powerful lessons I've learned is that the five LIGHT principles are not meant to stand alone. They are **interconnected**, balancing and strengthening one another.

- ❖ **Love** ensures that leadership is caring and compassionate, but without **Integrity**, love can become permissive.
- ❖ **Integrity** anchors truth and honesty, but without **Goodness**, it can feel rigid or harsh.
- ❖ **Goodness** builds people up and keeps the mission pure, but without **Humility**, it can slide into pride or self-righteousness.
- ❖ **Humility** creates trust and unity, but without **Transparency**, it can leave people guessing about decisions.
- ❖ **Transparency** strengthens trust, but without **Love**, it can turn into bluntness that wounds rather than heals.

Together, these principles create a leadership style that is **effective, compassionate, and sustainable**.

The Burden of Leadership vs. the Rest of LIGHT

Many leaders quietly carry the heavy weight of leadership. They wrestle with conflict among team members, the stress of making the right decisions, or the fear of disappointing others. In churches, this often leads to what we call "church hurt," where poor communication or unresolved conflict causes people to leave or withdraw. In workplaces, it leads to disengagement, turnover, or toxic environments.

The LIGHT Way is not about ignoring these challenges it is about addressing them with values that bring peace and restoration. Leaders who walk in LIGHT do not have to manipulate outcomes or worry constantly about people's reactions. They lead with clarity and peace of mind, knowing they are aligned with principles that honor God and respect people.

As Jesus said in Matthew 11:30: *"For my yoke is easy and my burden is light."* That promise echoes in this leadership model. When you lead with LIGHT, the weight is shared with God and guided by His Spirit.

A Personal Calling

When the Lord first impressed these five principles on my heart, I didn't see them as separate qualities to work on one at a time. He showed me how they work together like ingredients in a recipe or beams in a structure creating balance and strength.

I saw how leaders in churches, nonprofits, and workplaces were struggling with the same issues: communication breakdowns, lack of accountability, burnout, division, and mistrust. I knew there had to be a better way one that not only got the work done but also honored people and glorified God. The LIGHT principles became that way.

The Journey Ahead

This book will walk you through each principle in depth, showing how to apply it in your leadership role. Each chapter includes:

- ❖ A clear definition of the principle.
- ❖ Examples in **ministry and workplace** settings.
- ❖ **Barriers** that make the principle difficult to live out.
- ❖ **Practical steps** to help you grow.

- ❖ **Biblical anchors** that ground the principle in God's Word.
- ❖ **Reflection questions** to guide your personal application.

My prayer is that as you read, you will not only learn about the LIGHT Way but begin to **live it out** in your own leadership journey.

Reflection Questions

- ❖ Where in my leadership do I feel the heaviest burden right now?
- ❖ Do I tend to focus on results more than on people, or on people more than results?
- ❖ How might the LIGHT principles bring balance and rest to my leadership?

Space for Thoughts & Refresh

Take a few moments to breathe, reflect, and let the principle of this chapter settle into your spirit.

- ❖ What stood out to me most in this chapter was:

  _____

- ❖ Where I feel challenged to grow is:

  _____

- ❖ One truth or phrase I want to carry with me is:

  _____

Pause. Pray. Refresh.

Let this space serve as a reset before moving into your deeper journal reflections.

_____

_____

_____

CHAPTER 2

Love: Leading with Care and Clear Expectations

When most people hear the word *love* in leadership, they think of kindness, compassion, and encouragement. And those are important. But the kind of love required for LIGHT leadership goes deeper.

Love, in this context, means **valuing people enough to lead them well** which includes being clear about expectations, holding them accountable for outcomes, and helping them grow into their potential. True leadership love is not indulgence, nor is it neglect. It is a commitment to shepherding people with both **care and clarity**.

Jesus Himself modeled this. He washed His disciples' feet, showing humility and service (John 13:14). Yet He also corrected them, challenged their thinking, and held them accountable to their calling. Real love is not weak; it is strong enough to guide, teach, and, when needed, rebuke always for the sake of growth and unity.

Scripture Foundation

- ❖ *"My command is this: Love each other as I have loved you."* John 15:12
- ❖ *"Do everything in love."* 1 Corinthians 16:14
- ❖ *"The Lord disciplines the one he loves, and he chastens everyone he accepts as his son."* Hebrews 12:6
- ❖ *"Above all, love each other deeply, because love covers over a multitude of sins."* 1 Peter 4:8

These verses remind us that leadership love is both **tender and tough**. It encourages, but it also corrects. It builds people up without excusing behavior that tears others down.

What Love Looks Like in Leadership

- ❖ **Clear expectations:** Love sets people up for success by being upfront about what is needed and expected.
- ❖ **Encouragement and affirmation:** Love celebrates people's efforts and recognizes their value, even when they fall short.

- ❖ **Correction done with care:** Love doesn't avoid conflict; it addresses issues respectfully, aiming to restore rather than shame.
- ❖ **Making space for growth**: Love provides opportunities for volunteers and team members to try, fail, learn, and be supported.
- ❖ **Protecting the flock**: Love guards against harmful behaviors (gossip, division, mistreatment) by stepping in firmly when needed.

Case Example: Ushers Ministry Conflict

An usher shows up late three Sundays in a row.

- ❖ A leader driven only by compassion might overlook it, thinking, *"I don't want to hurt their feelings."*
- ❖ A harsh leader might scold them publicly, shaming them into compliance.
- ❖ But a **LIGHT leader guided by love** meets privately with the usher and says:

  "I value you and your ministry here, but when you arrive late, guests aren't welcomed the way we intend. How can we work together to improve this?"

This approach communicates care while upholding accountability.

The Pitfalls of Misunderstood Love

- ❖ **Avoidance** Mistaking love for "not rocking the boat" leaves issues unresolved.
- ❖ **Overindulgence** Allowing poor behavior to continue without correction undermines the team.
- ❖ **Harshness without care** Correcting without compassion breeds resentment and fear.
- ❖ **Conditional love** Showing kindness only when volunteers perform well creates insecurity.

Why Love Matters in Ministry

- ❖ **It creates safety:** Volunteers know they are valued as people, not just for their performance.
- ❖ **It fosters unity:** A culture of love breaks down cliques, competition, and bitterness.
- ❖ **It reflects Christ:** When leaders show love, the church becomes a living testimony of God's heart.
- ❖ **It strengthens commitment:** People stay when they feel cared for and guided with fairness.

Reflection Questions

1. Do I avoid necessary conversations in the name of "keeping the peace"?

2. Would those I lead describe me as encouraging and supportive?

3. When I correct others, is it done with love and restoration in mind?

4. Do I communicate expectations clearly, or do I leave people guessing?

5. Have I created an environment where people feel both cared for *and* challenged to grow?

Ministry Application

❖ **Set expectations early**: When assigning roles, explain clearly what success looks like.

❖ **Encourage publicly, correct privately**: Celebrate wins in front of others but handle corrections oneon-one.

❖ **Check your motives**: Before a hard conversation, ask, *"Am I doing this to prove a point or to help this person grow?"*

❖ **Model patience**: Give people room to learn. Growth takes time, and love provides that space.

❖ **Guard the team's unity**: Address gossip or division quickly, firmly, and lovingly.

Reflection Exercise: The Love + Accountability Balance

As a leader, it's not enough to be caring without being clear — and it's not enough to be clear without being caring. True leadership requires holding both **love and accountability** together.

Take a few moments to imagine yourself in the following situations:

Scenarios:

1. A volunteer regularly does not show up for their assigned time.

2. Someone dominates meetings and doesn't allow others to share.

3. Two team members are in ongoing conflict.

For each scenario, reflect on these questions:

- ❖ **What would avoidance look like?** (e.g., ignoring the problem, hoping it goes away)

- ❖ **What would harsh correction look like?** (e.g., being overly critical, shaming the person in front of others)

- ❖ **What would the LIGHT way of love look like?** (balancing care with clear expectations, showing compassion while still addressing the issue)

*Tip: Write down your responses below. Pay attention to where you naturally lean toward avoidance or harshness. Then consider how the LIGHT principle of **love** can guide you into a healthier balance.*

Prayer

"Lord, help me to lead with Your love a love that encourages, protects, and corrects. Give me the courage to have hard conversations with grace, and the wisdom to celebrate and guide those I serve. May my leadership reflect Your heart of truth and love."

Space for Thoughts & Refresh

Take a moment to pause and reflect on how *love* shows up in your leadership. Love is not indulgence, and it's not avoidance. It is care wrapped in clarity.

- ❖ What stood out most to me about love in leadership is:

  _____

  _____

  _____

- ❖ Where I feel challenged to balance care and clarity is:

  _____

  _____

  _____

- ❖ One way I can prevent church hurt through love is:

  _____

  _____

  _____

Pause. Pray. Refresh.

_____

_____

CHAPTER 3

Integrity: Leading with Wholeness

If love is the heart of leadership, **integrity** is its backbone. Without integrity, leadership collapses under the weight of inconsistency. Integrity is about wholeness living in such a way that your values, words, and actions align. It's not about perfection, but about consistency and trustworthiness.

Leaders with integrity don't need to announce it. People recognize it in the way they keep their word, make decisions, and treat others. Integrity shines brightest not in moments of applause but in the quiet spaces where choices are made when no one is watching, when the easier road tempts, when compromise could bring quick results but lasting damage.

What Integrity Really Means

The word "integrity" comes from the root *integer*, meaning "whole" or "undivided." An integrated life is one where there are no hidden compartments, no double standards, no masks. In leadership, integrity means:

- ❖ Being the same person in private as in public.
- ❖ Making decisions based on principle, not convenience.
- ❖ Following through on commitments, even when it's costly.
- ❖ Speaking the truth consistently, not just when it benefits you.

Integrity in Ministry and the Workplace

- ❖ **In Ministry:** Integrity looks like handling church finances with honesty, teaching without compromise, and ensuring that decisions are aligned with biblical truth. It means leaders do not say one thing from the pulpit and live another way in private. Integrity creates a culture where trust in leadership mirrors trust in God.
- ❖ **In the Workplace:** Integrity shows up in fair hiring practices, honest reporting, and making decisions that

reflect stated values. It also means being transparent about mistakes and addressing problems directly rather than hiding them.

When leaders walk in integrity, people know where they stand. They don't wonder if there's a hidden agenda, because words and actions line up.

The Cost of Compromise

Integrity is often tested in small ways. A little exaggeration in a report. A promise made but quietly broken. A shortcut taken because "no one will know." But small cracks, left unchecked, grow into gaping breaks.

Compromise might bring temporary relief, but it costs long-term trust. Once broken, trust is difficult to rebuild. That's why Proverbs 11:3 says: *"The integrity of the upright guides them, but the unfaithful are destroyed by their duplicity."*

A leader without integrity cannot guide effectively because people won't follow where there is no trust.

Barriers to Integrity

Even leaders with good intentions face challenges to integrity:

- ❖ **Pressure to Compromise:** The temptation to take shortcuts to meet goals.
- ❖ **Fear of Conflict:** Avoiding the truth to keep the peace.
- ❖ **Rationalization:** Excusing dishonesty as "small" or "necessary."
- ❖ **Weariness:** Losing discipline when leadership feels overwhelming.

Identifying these barriers helps leaders remain vigilant in protecting their integrity.

Practical Ways to Lead with Integrity

1. **Keep Your Word:** Say less if needed, but always follow through.
2. **Admit Mistakes Quickly:** People respect honesty more than cover-ups.
3. **Align Decisions with Values:** Filter choices through God's Word and organizational principles.
4. **Practice Transparency**: Share the reasoning behind decisions to build confidence and trust.
5. **Invite Accountability**: Surround yourself with people who will tell you the truth.

Biblical Anchor

Jesus taught in Matthew 5:37, *"Let your 'Yes' be yes, and your 'No,' no; anything beyond this comes from the evil one."* Integrity is about simple, steady faithfulness. It is about being trustworthy in word and deed.

Reflection Questions

- ❖ Where am I most tempted to compromise my integrity?
- ❖ Do those I lead trust me to follow through on what I say?
- ❖ How can I better align my words and actions this week?
- ❖ Who in my life can hold me accountable to walk in integrity?

Space for Thoughts & Refresh

Integrity is the strength of leadership. Like metal tested in fire, it proves itself in consistency.

❖ A place where my integrity feels strong is:

_____

_____

_____

❖ A place where my integrity is tested most often is:

_____

_____

_____

❖ One step I can take to walk more securely is:

_____

_____

_____

Pause. Pray. Refresh.

_____

_____

_____

CHAPTER 4

Goodness: Doing What is Right and Life-Giving

Goodness in LIGHT leadership is more than simply being a "nice person" or doing kind acts when convenient. It is an intentional commitment to doing what is right, beneficial, and life-giving even when it costs you something. Goodness is love and integrity in action. It is visible, demonstrated not just in words, but in consistent deeds, decisions, and the opportunities you create for others.

A leader who walks in goodness leaves people better than they found them spiritually, emotionally, and professionally.

What Goodness Looks Like in Leadership

Goodness means noticing people, valuing their contributions, and taking action to build them up.

It shows up when a leader:

- ❖ Recognizes someone's potential and gives them a chance to shine.
- ❖ Publicly credits others when recognition is due.
- ❖ Privately offers encouragement when someone feels like giving up.
- ❖ Shields their team from unnecessary harm or discouragement.
- ❖ Creates opportunities for growth and celebration rather than only pointing out flaws.

The opposite of goodness is **indifference** being so focused on your own success that you fail to lift others up. A LIGHT leader chooses to notice, affirm, and strengthen those around them.

Goodness with Discernment

Goodness doesn't mean saying "yes" to everything. Not every request or idea serves the mission well, and not every opportunity to act is truly beneficial. A wise leader evaluates what will produce the best for the most people while staying aligned with values and vision.

True goodness requires discernment: knowing when to step in, when to step back, and when to redirect energy toward what brings life.

Goodness in Ministry and the Workplace

❖ **In Ministry:** Goodness ensures ministry is not just effective, but edifying. It means protecting volunteers from burnout, shielding them from toxic interactions, and equipping them with what they need to thrive. It also means leading in a way that prevents "church hurt" scattering the flock through careless words, unchecked conflict, or neglect.

❖ **In the Workplace:** Goodness may look like trusting employees with meaningful tasks, celebrating team wins, and making ethical choices even when pressured otherwise. It creates a culture where people feel safe, valued, and motivated to give their best.

Goodness makes leadership not only productive, but life giving.

Barriers to Practicing Goodness

❖ **Busyness**: Being too rushed to notice the needs of others.

❖ **Fear of Perception**: Worrying that too much kindness will look like weakness.

❖ **Burnout**: Feeling too drained to go the extra mile for others.

❖ **Personal Offense**: Struggling to extend goodness when hurt by someone.

Goodness requires a deliberate choice to act with generosity of spirit, even when obstacles arise.

Practical Ways to Lead with Goodness

1. **Be Visible in Your Care**: Don't assume people know you value them; show it in action.

2. **Look for the Overlooked**: Pay attention to quiet contributors or those struggling silently.

3. **Align Goodness with Accountability**: Being good doesn't mean lowering standards; it means setting people up for success while expecting excellence.

4. **Create a Ripple Effect**: Model goodness so consistently that it becomes part of your team or ministry's culture.

Biblical Anchor

Micah 6:8 gives one of the clearest mandates for leaders: *"He has shown you, O mortal, what is good. And what does the Lord require of you? To act justly and to love mercy and to walk humbly with your God."*

Goodness is not optional for LIGHT leaders it is a required expression of our calling.

Reflection Questions

- ❖ In what ways is my leadership visibly good?
- ❖ Where have I relied more on good intentions than good actions?
- ❖ Who around me needs encouragement, recognition, or protection this week?
- ❖ How can I model goodness in a way that others will carry forward?

Space for Thoughts & Refresh

Goodness is not just what we feel it's what we *do*. It's leadership in action.

- ❖ A recent act of goodness I've experienced or witnessed is:

_____

_____

_____

- ❖ A person I can encourage or uplift this week is:

_____

_____

_____

- ❖ One way I can let goodness be visible in my deeds is:

_____

_____

_____

Pause. Pray. Refresh.

_____

_____

_____

CHAPTER 5

Humility: Leading with a Servant's Heart

Humility is one of the most misunderstood qualities in leadership. Some mistake it for weakness, insecurity, or lack of confidence. But in the LIGHT Way, humility is not weakness it is **strength under control**. It is the ability to lead with authority while serving with grace.

A humble leader doesn't need to prove their worth, demand recognition, or dominate conversations. Instead, they elevate others, steward their influence wisely, and acknowledge that every good gift comes from God.

Psalm 127:1 reminds us: *"Unless the Lord builds the house, the builders labor in vain."* Humility begins with recognizing that leadership is not about us it is about God's mission, God's people, and the good we are called to steward.

What Humility Looks Like in Leadership

A humble leader esteems others higher than themselves. They listen before speaking, welcome input, and honor contributions. They don't feel diminished when others succeed, they rejoice.

Humility is expressed when a leader:

- ❖ Rolls up their sleeves and works alongside their team, not above them.
- ❖ Freely gives credit where it is due.
- ❖ Asks for advice and seeks counsel, even from those "under" them.
- ❖ Admits mistakes and takes responsibility without excuses.

Humility doesn't diminish authority it enhances it. People trust and follow leaders who are approachable, teachable, and honest.

Humility in Ministry and the Workplace

- ❖ **In Ministry:** Humility reflects Christ Himself, who came not to be served but to serve (Mark 10:45). It means leading without pride of position and remembering that the people we lead are God's flock, not ours. A humble pastor or ministry leader creates unity and protects against division by modeling servanthood.

- ❖ **In the Workplace:** Humility looks like leaders who ask for feedback, admit when they don't know something, and empower employees to lead in their areas of strength. It fosters collaboration, creativity, and trust making the team stronger than any one individual.

The Power of Humility

Humility carries a unique power. It:

- ❖ **Diffuses conflict**: Pride escalates arguments, but humility softens hearts.
- ❖ **Strengthens relationships**: People bond deeply with leaders who listen and care.
- ❖ **Keeps focus on the mission**: Pride makes leadership about "me"; humility makes it about the greater purpose.
- ❖ **Protects the leader's heart**: Humility guards against arrogance, entitlement, and self-promotion.

True humility doesn't mean thinking less of yourself it means thinking of yourself less.

Barriers to Humility

Even strong leaders struggle with humility at times:

- ❖ **Pride in Success**: Believing past wins mean you no longer need input.
- ❖ **Fear of Losing Control**: Worrying that humility will make you look weak.
- ❖ **Comparison**: Measuring yourself against others instead of God's calling.
- ❖ **Insecurity**: Overcompensating with arrogance or defensiveness.

Recognizing these barriers keeps us grounded and dependent on God's grace.

Practical Ways to Lead with Humility

1. **Ask More Questions Than You Answer:** Create space for others' voices.
2. **Share the Spotlight**: Publicly recognize team contributions.
3. **Admit When You're Wrong:** Model repentance and accountability.
4. **Serve in Small Ways:** Take on tasks beneath your title as a visible act of service.
5. **Seek Feedback Regularly**: Invite others to sharpen your leadership.

Biblical Anchor

James 4:10 says, *"Humble yourselves before the Lord, and He will lift you up."*

In God's kingdom, the way up is down. Humility positions us for God's promotion because it keeps our hearts aligned with His purposes.

Reflection Questions

 ❖ Do I esteem others higher than myself in action, not just intention?

 ❖ How do I respond to feedback defensive or teachable?

 ❖ Where am I tempted to lead from pride instead of servanthood?

 ❖ What one act of visible humility can I practice this week?

Space for Thoughts & Refresh

Humility is not weakness; it's strength under control. It is about choosing to serve rather than being served.

❖ A moment I have seen humility transform a situation is:

_____

_____

_____

❖ A place where pride might hinder my leadership is:

_____

_____

_____

❖ One way I can model servant leadership this week is:

_____

_____

_____

Pause. Pray. Refresh.

_____

_____

_____

CHAPTER 6

Transparency: Leading with Openness and Trust

Transparency is the open window of leadership. It allows people to see not just what you do, but why you do it. A transparent leader communicates clearly, shares decisions openly, and owns both successes and failures.

Transparency doesn't weaken authority it strengthens trust. When people know they can count on you to tell the truth, they will follow with confidence, even when the path is difficult. But when communication is vague, hidden, or inconsistent, suspicion and uncertainty quickly grow.

What Transparency Really Means

Transparency is not about telling everything to everyone. It is about creating an environment of **clarity and openness** where people are not left in the dark.

A transparent leader:

- ❖ Explains the "why" behind decisions, not just the "what."
- ❖ Shares progress including challenges rather than hiding reality.
- ❖ Communicates consistently, avoiding secrecy that breeds mistrust.
- ❖ Admits limitations and mistakes instead of pretending to have all the answers.

Like a clear glass window, transparency lets truth and light pass through without distortion or manipulation.

Transparency in Ministry and the Workplace

- ❖ **In Ministry:** Transparency builds trust in leaders and protects the church from division. It looks like communicating changes clearly, being upfront about ministry needs, explaining stewardship decisions, and owning mistakes with humility. It prevents "church hurt" by removing shadows of secrecy and fostering honest, healthy conversations.

- ❖ **In the Workplace:** Transparency strengthens engagement and loyalty. It shows up in sharing company goals and updates, explaining why changes are made, and giving straightforward feedback. Transparent leaders don't let rumors fill the silence they lead with clear and honest communication.

Transparency Requires Humility

Transparency and humility walk hand in hand. To be transparent, a leader must be willing to say:

- ❖ "I don't know."
- ❖ "I made a mistake."
- ❖ "We need to change direction."

Far from weakening credibility, this honesty builds trust. People respect leaders who admit reality and invite others to walk with them in it.

Barriers to Transparency

- ❖ **Fear of Criticism**: Worrying that being open will invite pushback.
- ❖ **Desire for Control**: Believing secrecy makes it easier to keep people compliant.
- ❖ **Uncertainty**: Not wanting to admit when the path ahead is unclear.
- ❖ **Cultural Habits**: Leading in environments where "closed doors" are the norm.

These barriers can be overcome with courage and commitment to trust-building.

Practical Ways to Lead with Transparency
1. **Explain the "Why" Before the "What"**: Help people understand the reasoning behind decisions.

2. **Keep Communication Flowing**: Provide regular updates to prevent rumors.

3. **Own Decisions and Mistakes**: Take responsibility instead of hiding behind others.

4. **Create Safe Spaces for Dialogue**: Invite questions and honest feedback.

5. **Model Honesty in Small Things**: Daily transparency builds trust for big moments.

Biblical Anchor
2 Corinthians 8:21 says, *"For we aim at what is honorable not only in the Lord's sight but also in the sight of man."*
Transparency is about walking honorably before both God and people keeping motives clear and actions consistent.

Reflection Questions
- ❖ Do those I lead understand not just my decisions, but my reasons?
- ❖ Have I withheld information out of fear instead of wisdom?

❖ How can I create more opportunities for honest dialogue?

❖ What's one step I can take this week to model transparency more clearly?

Space for Thoughts & Refresh

Transparency is the clarity that lets light pass through.

When our leadership is clear, people can see Christ in us.

❖ An area of my leadership that feels "clear glass" is:

_____

_____

_____

❖ An area that feels "cloudy" and needs attention is:

_____

_____

_____

❖ One action I can take to keep my leadership transparent is:

_____

_____

_____

Pause. Pray. Refresh.

_____

_____

_____

WHAT CAN DERAIL A LIGHT LEADER

You've now walked through the five LIGHT principles — **Love, Integrity, Goodness, Humility, and Transparency.**

These are the windows that allow God's light to shine through our leadership. When kept clear, they build trust, unity, and strength in every ministry and workplace.

But leadership is not only about what we *do right*. It is also about recognizing the pitfalls that can weaken our influence when we drift from these values. Even the strongest leader can stumble if blind spots go unchecked.

That's why it's important to pause here and look honestly at **what can derail a LIGHT leader.**

The following ten derailers are not theoretical — they are the real traps leaders face every day:

- ❖ Pride creeping in when success comes.
- ❖ Avoidance when accountability is needed.
- ❖ Words that wound instead of heal.
- ❖ Or simply forgetting to love in the name of "getting things done."

By naming these derailers, we shine light into the shadows. We can learn to spot them quickly, confess when we've slipped, and realign with the LIGHT principles.

So before moving to the conclusion of this journey, let's take a deep breath and examine the **10 common derailers** that every leader must guard against.

"So, if you think you are standing firm, be careful that you don't fall." — 1 Corinthians 10:12

THINGS THAT WILL DERAIL A LIGHT LEADER

Derailer 1: Hoarding Credit

Taking recognition for yourself while ignoring others' contributions.

Scripture Anchor

"Do nothing out of selfish ambition or vain conceit. Rather, in humility value others above yourselves." — Philippians 2:3

Teaching/Story

At an outreach event, one leader accepted all the praise for a successful day, forgetting the team who had set up, served, and cleaned. Volunteers felt unseen. A LIGHT leader makes it a habit to spread gratitude and shine the spotlight on others.

Reflection Questions

- ❖ When did I last publicly acknowledge my team's contributions?
- ❖ Do I secretly crave recognition more than giving it away?
- ❖ How can I build a culture of gratitude this week?

Derailer 2: Micromanaging

Refusing to delegate or trust others, which stifles growth and creativity.

Scripture Anchor

"Moses' father-in-law replied, 'What you are doing is not good… You will wear yourselves out. The work is too heavy for you; you cannot handle it alone.'" — Exodus 18:17–18

Teaching/Story

Pastor Daniel insisted on doing every detail himself. His volunteers felt unnecessary and eventually stopped showing up. Delegation is not weakness — it's wisdom. LIGHT leaders equip and trust others, creating space for gifts to flourish.

Reflection Questions

❖ Do I hoard tasks out of fear they won't be done "my way"?

❖ Who can I release into greater responsibility this week?

❖ How would my load lighten if I trusted my team more?

Derailer 3: Inconsistency

Saying one thing but doing another, eroding integrity and trust.

Scripture Anchor

"Let your 'Yes' be 'Yes,' and your 'No,' 'No.'" — Matthew 5:37

Teaching/Story

A leader promised monthly training but never followed through. Volunteers became discouraged and mistrust grew. LIGHT leaders know that consistency — even in small promises — is the backbone of integrity. **Reflection Questions**

- ❖ Where have I promised too much and delivered too little?
- ❖ Do my actions match the words I speak?
- ❖ What is one area I need to bring back into alignment?

Derailer 4: Lack of Transparency

Withholding information, hiding motives, or creating confusion.

Scripture Anchor

"For we aim at what is honorable not only in the Lord's sight but also in the sight of man." — 2 Corinthians 8:21

Teaching/Story

A church board decided to shift ministries but never explained the reasoning. The secrecy fueled rumors and division. Transparency doesn't mean oversharing; it means explaining clearly so people aren't left in the dark.

Reflection Questions

- ❖ Do those I lead understand both my decisions and my reasons?
- ❖ What have I been tempted to keep hidden?
- ❖ What one step can I take toward more open communication?

Derailer 5: Pride and Ego

Needing to be the center of attention instead of allowing others to shine.

Scripture Anchor

"Humble yourselves before the Lord, and he will lift you up."
— James 4:10

Teaching/Story

One leader insisted on making every announcement and leading every prayer. Team members felt like spectators instead of servants. Pride isolates; humility multiplies influence. LIGHT leaders gladly step aside so others can grow.

Reflection Questions

- ❖ Do I rejoice when others succeed, or do I feel threatened?
- ❖ How often do I step aside to let others lead?
- ❖ Where do I need to choose humility over self promotion?

Derailer 6: Neglecting Love

Leading without care, compassion, or genuine regard for the people you serve.

Scripture Anchor

"Above all, love each other deeply, because love covers over a multitude of sins." — 1 Peter 4:8

Teaching/Story

A leader focused only on results, overlooking the exhaustion of their volunteers. Over time, resentment built up. LIGHT leaders pause to care, check in, and protect their team's well-being. Love fuels longevity.

Reflection Questions

- ❖ Do I prioritize tasks over people?
- ❖ When was the last time I checked in on my team personally?

- ❖ How can I better show love through both care and clarity?

Derailer 7: Avoiding Accountability

Refusing to admit mistakes or accept responsibility for failures.

Scripture Anchor

"Whoever conceals their sins does not prosper, but the one who confesses and renounces them finds mercy." — Proverbs 28:13

Teaching/Story

When a project failed, a leader blamed volunteers instead of admitting they had miscommunicated. Trust crumbled. LIGHT leaders own their part, apologize when necessary, and set the example of accountability. **Reflection Questions**

- ❖ When I make a mistake, do I admit it or shift the blame?
- ❖ Who models accountability in my life and leadership?
- ❖ What one area do I need to take responsibility for today?

Derailer 8: Favoritism

Elevating certain people while overlooking or dismissing others.

Scripture Anchor

"My brothers and sisters, believers in our glorious Lord Jesus Christ must not show favoritism." — James 2:1

Teaching/Story

In a ministry, the same volunteers were always chosen for visible roles. Others quietly stopped serving because they felt unseen. LIGHT leaders look for overlooked gifts and ensure fairness.

Reflection Questions

- ❖ Do I gravitate toward certain people while ignoring others?
- ❖ Who in my team needs encouragement or opportunity right now?
- ❖ How can I ensure all feel valued and respected?

Derailer 9: Ignoring Feedback

Rejecting constructive input that could improve your leadership.

Scripture Anchor

"The way of fools seems right to them, but the wise listen to advice." — Proverbs 12:15

Teaching/Story

A leader dismissed concerns about long meetings, saying, "This is how we've always done it." Volunteers disengaged. LIGHT leaders invite feedback, even when it stings, and use it to grow.

Reflection Questions

❖ Do I welcome feedback, or do I become defensive?

❖ Who do I trust to speak truth into my leadership?

❖ What feedback have I been avoiding but need to hear?

Derailer 10: Causing Church Hurt / Workplace Hurt

Speaking harshly, belittling others, or using position to wound rather than build.

Scripture Anchor

"Do not let any unwholesome talk come out of your mouths, but only what is helpful for building others up." — Ephesians 4:29

Teaching/Story

A leader publicly scolded a volunteer, leaving them humiliated. That volunteer never returned. LIGHT leaders correct with care, address issues privately, and ensure their words heal rather than harm.

Reflection Questions

- ❖ Do my words build up or tear down those I lead?
- ❖ When was the last time I corrected in private instead of public?
- ❖ What step can I take to prevent "church hurt" in my team?

Reminder:

A LIGHT leader doesn't dim others to shine brighter. True leadership multiplies the light so the whole team can shine together.

CONCLUSION ~ KEEP THE LIGHT FLOWING

L eadership is a sacred trust. Whether in ministry, the workplace, or the community, the way we lead shapes lives, influences faith, and impacts futures. That's why the LIGHT principles Love, **Integrity, Goodness, Humility, and Transparency** are more than ideas. They are windows that must be kept clear so the light of our leadership can shine.

The Windows of Leadership

Think again of the picture we began with: leadership as light shining through a series of windows. Each window represents one of the five principles. If even one pane is clouded if love is absent, integrity is compromised, goodness is neglected, humility is forgotten, or transparency is hidden the light is distorted. The mission suffers, people stumble, and the leader feels the crushing weight of mistrust and confusion.

But when the panes are clean and aligned, the light flows freely. The path is illuminated. People walk together with confidence and unity. And the leader rests easier, knowing they have led well, with a clear heart and a steady hand.

The Ongoing Work of Leadership

But here is the truth: leadership is not a one-time act of cleaning the windows. Over time, pressures, disappointments, misunderstandings, and personal weaknesses can cloud even the clearest glass. That's why LIGHT leadership requires **intentional maintenance**.

It means regularly asking ourselves:

- ❖ Am I leading with love, or have I slipped into avoidance or favoritism?
- ❖ Am I walking in integrity, or have I allowed small compromises to creep in?
- ❖ Am I demonstrating goodness, or just assuming people know I care?
- ❖ Am I practicing humility, or letting pride and comparison shape my choices?
- ❖ Am I being transparent, or hiding truths out of fear or control?

The LIGHT Way calls us to return to these principles again and again to realign when necessary, to confess when we've fallen short, and to renew our commitment to lead in ways that honor God and serve people.

The Legacy of LIGHT Leadership

Leadership is not only about what we achieve; it is about who we become and how we influence others along the way. When you lead with LIGHT:

- ❖ People grow instead of wither.
- ❖ Teams unite instead of fracture.
- ❖ Missions move forward without leaving wounded people behind.
- ❖ Leaders rest at night with peace instead of anxiety.

For me, this truth is personal. My mother often said, *"I've got my beans on in my mama's pot."* At first, I thought it was about food. But it was never really about beans cooking on the stove. It was about something much deeper the strength, resilience, and faith passed down from one generation to the next.

That "pot" was a vessel of legacy. It carried wisdom, prayer, endurance, and faith seasoned through hardship and perseverance. Just as beans simmer slowly until they are ready to nourish, my mother's life was a long, slow testimony of patience and love. She showed us, day by day, that with God's strength we could keep going, keep believing, and keep loving, no matter what came our way.

That is the essence of **LIGHT leadership**. It creates a culture where people are not drained, but strengthened. It feeds souls with encouragement, steadies teams with consistency, and sustains ministries with faithfulness.

And like my mama's pot, LIGHT leadership lingers long after the moment has passed. Its aroma fills the atmosphere. Its influence nourishes lives. And its strength passes on to future generations.

So I leave you with this: when you lead the LIGHT Way, you are not just guiding a team or completing a mission you are leaving a legacy. A legacy of love, integrity, goodness, humility, and transparency. A legacy that lights the path for others and lightens the load for yourself.

Final Charge

As you step forward from these pages, remember this: leadership is not about titles, positions, or applause. It is about how you show up, day after day, with the LIGHT of Christ guiding your steps. Lead with **Love** that sets clear expectations and cares deeply. Walk in **Integrity** that remains steady under pressure. Practice **Goodness** that is visible in action, not just intention. Embrace **Humility** that serves and lifts others higher. And live with **Transparency** that lets the light of Christ shine clearly through you.

Go and lead the LIGHT Way not perfectly, but faithfully. May your leadership light the path for those you serve, and may it lighten your load so you can rest with peace and joy. And may the legacy of your leadership, like the aroma of Mama's pot, nourish generations to come.

MOVING FROM LEARNING TO LIVING

You've walked through the five LIGHT principles **Love, Integrity, Goodness, Humility, and Transparency.** You've reflected, prayed, and captured thoughts along the way.

Now it's time to put these truths into practice. Growth happens through repetition, reflection, and intentional action. The following **30-Day Journal** is designed to help you:

❖ Deepen what you've learned in each chapter.

❖ Build daily habits that reflect LIGHT leadership.

❖ Track your growth as you live this out step by step.

Take your time. Write honestly. Don't rush. Each day is an opportunity to **light the path for others and lighten your own load.**

HOW TO USE THIS JOURNAL

This 30-Day Journal is designed to help you move from **learning** to **living** the LIGHT Way of leadership. Over the next thirty days, you'll reflect on scripture, apply the principles, and record how God is shaping you as a leader.

Daily Flow

Each day follows the same pattern:

- ❖ **Date Line**: write the date to track your journey.
- ❖ **Scripture for Today**: begin with God's Word as your foundation.
- ❖ **Reflection Prompt**: pause to consider how the principle applies to your leadership.
- ❖ **My Reflection**: write honestly about your thoughts, experiences, and challenges.
- ❖ **Action Step for Today**: commit to one practical way you will live this out.
- ❖ **Prayer**: a short prayer to center your heart and invite God's help.

Tips for Success

- ❖ **Take your time:** Don't rush. Ten quiet minutes a day can transform how you lead.

- ❖ **Be honest:** Write openly this journal is between you and God.
- ❖ **Stay consistent:** Try to journal at the same time each day to build a habit.
- ❖ **Review often:** At the end of each week, look back at your reflections to notice growth.
- ❖ **Pray as you go:** Ask the Holy Spirit to guide your words and actions.

The Goal

By the end of these 30 days, you will not only understand the LIGHT principles more deeply you will have **practiced them daily**. You'll see how leading with **Love, Integrity, Goodness, Humility, and Transparency** lights the path for those you serve and lightens your own load as a leader.

30~DAY LIGHT JOURNAL

A Daily Practice of Reflection, Action, and Commitment

Day 1 ~ Love

Date: ——————————————

Scripture: 1 Peter 1:22 *"Love one another deeply, from the heart."*

Reflection Prompt:

How can I show genuine love to someone I lead today?

_____
_____
_____
_____

_____

Action Step:

Write a note or text of encouragement to one volunteer.

_____
_____
_____

_____

Commitment:

Today, I choose to lead with love by valuing people above

_____
_____

_____

Day 2 ~ Love

Date: ───────────────

Scripture: John 13:34 *"As I have loved you, so you must love one another."*

Reflection Prompt:

Do I correct with care or with frustration?

_____

_____

_____

_____

_____

Action Step:

Offer gentle correction privately to someone who needs guidance.

_____

_____

_____

_____

Commitment:

Today, I will love by speaking the truth in grace.

_____

_____

_____

_____

Day 3 ~ Love

Date: ————————————

Scripture: Romans 12:10 *"Be devoted to one another in love. Honor one another above yourselves."*

Reflection Prompt:

Who in my team needs more honor and recognition?

_____

_____

_____

_____

_____

Action Step:

Publicly affirm one person's contribution.

_____

_____

_____

_____

Commitment:

Today, I will love by honoring others openly.

_____

_____

_____

_____

Day 4 ~ Love

Date: ————————————————

Scripture: Colossians 3:14 *"And over all these virtues put on love, which binds them all together in perfect unity."*

Reflection Prompt:

Is there a strained relationship I've avoided addressing?

———————————————————————————
———————————————————————————
———————————————————————————
———————————————————————————
———————————————————————————

Action Step:

Take one step toward reconciliation.

———————————————————————————
———————————————————————————
———————————————————————————
———————————————————————————

Commitment:

Today, I will choose love that restores unity.

———————————————————————————
———————————————————————————
———————————————————————————
———————————————————————————

Day 5 ~ Love

Date: —————————————

Scripture: Proverbs 10:12 *"Hatred stirs up conflict, but love covers over all wrongs."*

Reflection Prompt:

Do I hold onto offenses or release them?

_____

_____

_____

_____

_____

Action Step:

Forgive someone in prayer and release the hurt.

_____

_____

_____

_____

Commitment:

Today, I will let love cover and heal offenses.

_____

_____

_____

_____

Day 6 ~ Love

Date: ──────────────

Scripture: 1 Corinthians 16:14 *"Do everything in love."*

Reflection Prompt:

How do I show love in the small tasks of leadership?

_____

_____

_____

_____

_____

Action Step:

Add a personal touch of kindness to something routine.

_____

_____

_____

_____

Commitment:

Today, I will love in every word and action.

_____

_____

_____

_____

Day 7 ~ Integrity

Date: _____

Scripture: Proverbs 11:3 *"The integrity of the upright guides them."*

Reflection Prompt:

Where do my words and actions need to align?

_____

_____

_____

_____

_____

Action Step:

Follow through on one small promise.

_____

_____

_____

_____

Commitment:

Today, I will let integrity guide my steps.

_____

_____

_____

_____

Day 8 ~ Integrity

Date: ───────────────

Scripture: Matthew 5:37 *"Let your 'Yes' be 'Yes,' and your 'No,' 'No.'"*

Reflection Prompt:

Do I say yes too quickly, then struggle to follow through?

_____

_____

_____

_____

_____

Action Step:

Say no to one thing today to protect your integrity.

_____

_____

_____

_____

Commitment:

Today, I will speak with honesty and clarity.

_____

_____

_____

_____

Day 9 ~ Integrity

Date: ───────────────

Scripture: Proverbs 10:9 *"Whoever walks in integrity walks securely."*

Reflection Prompt:

Do others feel secure in my leadership?

_____

_____

_____

_____

_____

Action Step:

Review one ministry process for honesty and transparency.

_____

_____

_____

_____

Commitment:

Today, I will build trust by walking securely in integrity.

_____

_____

_____

_____

Day 10 ~ Integrity

Date: _____

Scripture: Psalm 25:21 *"May integrity and uprightness protect me."*

Reflection Prompt:

When have I been tempted to cut corners?

_____

_____

_____

_____

_____

Action Step:

Correct one small thing you've left undone.

_____

_____

_____

_____

Commitment:

Today, I will let integrity protect my witness.

_____

_____

_____

_____

Day 11 ~ Integrity

Date: ──────────────

Scripture: Proverbs 28:6 *"Better the poor whose walk is blameless than the rich whose ways are perverse."*

Reflection Prompt:

Do I ever compromise values for convenience?

_____

_____

_____

_____

_____

Action Step:

Choose the harder but honest path in one decision.

_____

_____

_____

_____

Commitment:

Today, I will choose integrity over convenience.

_____

_____

_____

_____

Day 12 ~ Integrity

Date: ─────────────────

Scripture: Luke 16:10 *"Whoever can be trusted with very little can also be trusted with much."*

Reflection Prompt:

Am I faithful in small responsibilities?

_____

_____

_____

_____

_____

Action Step:

Be intentional in one small task today.

_____

_____

_____

_____

Commitment:

Today, I will prove faithful in the little things.

_____

_____

_____

_____

Day 13 ~ Goodness

Date: ───────────────

Scripture: Galatians 6:9 *"Let us not become weary in doing good."*

Reflection Prompt:

What good am I tempted to neglect?

_____

_____

_____

_____

_____

Action Step:

Do one act of kindness for a team member.

_____

_____

_____

_____

Commitment:

Today, I will not grow weary in doing good.

_____

_____

_____

_____

Day 14 ~ Goodness

Date: ————————————

Scripture: Romans 12:21 *"Do not be overcome by evil, but overcome evil with good."*

Reflection Prompt:

Am I reacting to negativity with frustration or goodness?

_____

_____

_____

_____

_____

Action Step:

Respond kindly in a tense situation today.

_____

_____

_____

_____

Commitment:

Today, I will overcome negativity with goodness.

_____

_____

_____

_____

Day 15 ~ Goodness

Date: ───────────────

Scripture: Psalm 23:6 *"Surely your goodness and love will follow me all the days of my life."*

Reflection Prompt:

Do people experience God's goodness through me?

_____

_____

_____

_____

_____

Action Step:

Offer unexpected encouragement to someone struggling.

_____

_____

_____

_____

Commitment:

Today, I will let God's goodness flow through me.

_____

_____

_____

_____

Day 16 ~ Goodness

Date: ───────────────

Scripture: Micah 6:8 *"Act justly, love mercy, and walk humbly with your God."*

Reflection Prompt:

Where can I be more fair and merciful in leadership?

_____

_____

_____

_____

_____

Action Step:

Mediate one situation with fairness and kindness.

_____

_____

_____

_____

Commitment:

Today, I will do good by acting justly and mercifully.

_____

_____

_____

_____

Day 17 ~ Goodness

Date: ───────────────

Scripture: Ephesians 2:10 *"We are God's handiwork, created in Christ Jesus to do good works."*

Reflection Prompt:

Am I intentional about the good works God prepared for me?

_____

_____

_____

_____

_____

Action Step:

Plan one specific good work today.

_____

_____

_____

_____

Commitment:

Today, I will walk in the good God has prepared for me.

_____

_____

_____

_____

Day 18 ~ Goodness

Date: ───────────────

Scripture: Hebrews 13:16 *"Do not forget to do good and to share with others, for with such sacrifices God is pleased."*

Reflection Prompt:

Do I share generously with others?

_____

_____

_____

_____

_____

Action Step:

Give of your time, resources, or encouragement.

_____

_____

_____

_____

Commitment:

Today, I will do good by sharing generously.

_____

_____

_____

_____

Day 19 ~ Humility

Date: ————————————————

Scripture: Philippians 2:3 *"Do nothing out of selfish ambition or vain conceit. Rather, in humility value others above yourselves."*

Reflection Prompt:

Do I see myself as more important than others?

_____

_____

_____

_____

_____

Action Step:

Put someone else's idea before your own today.

_____

_____

_____

_____

Commitment:

Today, I will honor others through humility.

_____

_____

_____

_____

Day 20 ~ Humility

Date: ─────────────────

Scripture: Matthew 23:12 *"For those who exalt themselves will be humbled, and those who humble themselves will be exalted."*

Reflection Prompt:

Do I seek recognition for serving?

_____

_____

_____

_____

_____

Action Step:

Serve in one way today where no one sees.

_____

_____

_____

_____

Commitment:

Today, I will choose humility over pride.

_____

_____

_____

_____

Day 21 ~ Humility

Date:

Scripture: James 4:1 *"Humble yourselves before the Lord, and he will lift you up."*

Reflection Prompt:

Where do I need to yield control to God?

_____

_____

_____

_____

_____

Action Step:

Pray specifically to surrender one area of your leadership to Him.

_____

_____

_____

_____

Commitment:

Today, I will humble myself before the Lord.

_____

_____

_____

_____

Day 22 ~ Humility

Date: ───────────────

Scripture: John 3:30 *"He must become greater; I must become less."*

Reflection Prompt:

Am I pointing people to Christ or to myself?

_____

_____

_____

_____

_____

Action Step:

Redirect praise back to God today.

_____

_____

_____

_____

Commitment:

Today, I will magnify Christ, not myself.

_____

_____

_____

_____

Day 23 ~ Humility

Date: ───────────────

Scripture: Matthew 20:26 *"Whoever wants to become great among you must be your servant."*

Reflection Prompt:

How am I serving others in love?

_____

_____

_____

_____

_____

Action Step:

Do one servant-hearted act without announcement.

_____

_____

_____

_____

Commitment:

Today, I will lead by serving others.

_____

_____

_____

_____

Day 24 ~ Humility

Date: ─────────────────

Scripture: 1 Peter 5:6 *"Humble yourselves, therefore, under God's mighty hand, that he may lift you up in due time."*

Reflection Prompt:

Where do I resist submitting to God's timing?

_____

_____

_____

_____

_____

Action Step:

Acknowledge His timing in prayer and release control.

_____

_____

_____

_____

Commitment:

Today, I will trust God's timing through humility.

_____

_____

_____

_____

Day 25 ~ Transparency

Date: _____

Scripture: Ephesians 4:25 *"Therefore each of you must put off falsehood and speak truthfully to your neighbor, for we are all members of one body."*

Reflection Prompt:

Am I avoiding a needed truth?

_____

_____

_____

_____

_____

Action Step:

Speak honestly to one person today in love.

_____

_____

_____

_____

Commitment:

Today, I will practice transparency in truth.

_____

_____

_____

_____

Day 26 ~ Transparency

Date: ────────────────

Scripture: 2 Corinthians 8:21 *"For we are taking pains to do what is right, not only in the eyes of the Lord but also in the eyes of man."*

Reflection Prompt:

Am I clear in explaining decisions?

_____

_____

_____

_____

_____

Action Step:

Share the "why" behind one decision today.

_____

_____

_____

_____

Commitment:

Today, I will lead with openness and clarity.

_____

_____

_____

_____

Day 27 ~ Transparency

Date: ——————————————————

Scripture: Proverbs 12:22 *"The Lord detests lying lips, but he delights in people who are trustworthy."*

Reflection Prompt:

Do others trust my words and actions?

_____

_____

_____

_____

_____

Action Step:

Reassure your team with honesty today.

_____

_____

_____

_____

Commitment:

Today, I will strengthen trust through transparency.

_____

_____

_____

_____

Day 28 ~ Transparency

Date:

Scripture: Ephesians 4:15 *"Instead, speaking the truth in love, we will grow to become in every respect the mature body of him who is the head, that is, Christ."*

Reflection Prompt:

Do I balance truth with grace?

_____

_____

_____

_____

_____

Action Step:

Have one honest, kind conversation.

_____

_____

_____

_____

Commitment:

Today, I will build trust through truthful love.

_____

_____

_____

_____

Day 29 ~ Transparency

Date: ──────────────────

Scripture: James 5:16 *"Therefore confess your sins to each other and pray for each other so that you may be healed."*

Reflection Prompt:

Do I admit my weaknesses openly?

_____

_____

_____

_____

_____

Action Step:

Share one struggle with a trusted peer for prayer.

_____

_____

_____

_____

Commitment:

Today, I will be transparent in my weaknesses.

_____

_____

_____

_____

Day 30 ~ Transparency

Date: _____

Scripture: Matthew 5:16 *"Let your light shine before others, that they may see your good deeds and glorify your Father in heaven."*

Reflection Prompt:

How is my transparency pointing others to Christ?

_____

_____

_____

_____

_____

Action Step:

Share one testimony of God's faithfulness today.

_____

_____

_____

_____

Commitment:

Today, I will shine the LIGHT of Christ through openness.

_____

_____

_____

_____

COMPLETION REFLECTION: MY LIGHT JOURNEY

Congratulations! You've completed 30 days of living and journaling the LIGHT Way. Take time to reflect on what God has done in you through this journey.

Looking Back

❖ The principle I grew the most in was:

_____

❖ The biggest shift I noticed in my leadership was:

_____

❖ One scripture that became especially meaningful to me was:

_____

Looking Forward

❖ One area I still want to grow in is:

_____

❖ One person I want to intentionally lead the LIGHT Way with is:

_____

❖ My prayer for my leadership going forward is:

_____

My Commitment

"I commit to leading with Love, Integrity, Goodness, Humility, and Transparency. With God's help, I will continue to light the path for those I serve and lighten the load for myself and others."

Signature: —————————————————————

Date: ———————————————————————

APPENDICES

(Optional Resources for Ministry and Workplace Leaders)

Choosing the Right Application

Leadership looks different depending on where you serve. Some of us lead in **churches and ministries**, while others lead in **nonprofits, schools, or workplaces**. The principles of LIGHT apply everywhere — but the way we honor those who lead us may vary.

That's why this appendix includes **two parallel sections**:

- ❖ **Honoring Our Shepherds** — written especially for those serving in churches or ministries.

- ❖ **Honoring Our Supervisors and Managers** — written for those serving in workplaces, nonprofits, or organizational settings. Choose the section that best fits your current context. Or, if you serve in both ministry and professional settings, reflect on how the LIGHT principles can guide you in *both*.

Wherever you lead — and wherever you follow — remember that **honor lightens the load** of those above us and strengthens the teams we are part of.

APPENDIX A HONORING OUR SHEPHERDS

Honoring Our Shepherds

Pastors carry a weight that few people truly understand. As under-shepherds of Jesus, they are entrusted with preaching the Word, guiding ministries, and caring for souls. While many see their pulpit moments and celebrations, they also carry unseen burdens: praying through the night, walking members through crisis, and bearing grief when people leave hurt or disappointed. Scripture reminds us:

❖ *"How beautiful are the feet of those who bring good news."* — Romans 10:15

❖ *"Obey your leaders and submit to them, for they are keeping watch over your souls, as those who will have to give an account. Let them do this with joy and not with groaning."* — Hebrews 13:17

As LIGHT leaders, one of our callings is to **support those who lead us.** We do this when we:

❖ Love them enough to pray, encourage, and not add to their burden.

- ❖ Walk in Integrity by keeping our word and supporting their vision.
- ❖ Demonstrate Goodness through acts of service and joyful participation.
- ❖ Show Humility by respecting their role as God's appointed shepherds.
- ❖ Live with Transparency by being open, honest, and trustworthy.

When we lead this way, we not only lighten our pastors' load but also bring joy to the heart of God.

Prayer for Our Shepherds

"Lord, we thank You for the shepherds You have placed over our lives. Strengthen them when they are weary, refresh them when they are burdened, and remind them that their work is not in vain. Guard their hearts from discouragement and hurt. Help us, as leaders, to support them with love, integrity, goodness, humility, and transparency, so their load is lighter and their joy is full. In Jesus' name, Amen."

Reflection

- ❖ One way I can encourage my pastor this week is:

  _____

- ❖ A habit I can build to support my shepherd consistently is:

  _____

APPENDIX B HONORING OUR SUPERVISORS

Honoring Our Supervisors and Managers

Every organization has leaders who carry responsibilities that most people never see. Supervisors and managers are tasked with balancing goals, supporting teams, making decisions under pressure, and often absorbing the weight of organizational challenges.

While employees may notice deadlines, meetings, or performance reviews, leaders are also navigating behind-the-scenes stressors: budget pressures, board expectations, and the responsibility of ensuring both people and mission succeed.

As LIGHT leaders, we are called to support those placed in authority over us. When we honor and encourage our supervisors, we strengthen the health of the entire workplace.

Scripture Anchor (universal leadership principle) *"Give to everyone what you owe them... if respect, then respect; if honor, then honor."* — Romans 13:7

We can apply the LIGHT principles upward in the workplace by:

- ❖ **Love**: Treating supervisors with respect and empathy, recognizing they are people with pressures of their own.
- ❖ **Integrity**: Following through on commitments, deadlines, and responsibilities.
- ❖ **Goodness**: Anticipating needs, offering solutions, and contributing positively to the team culture.
- ❖ **Humility**: Receiving feedback without defensiveness and valuing their experience.
- ❖ **Transparency**: Communicating openly and honestly to build trust.

When we live this way, we not only strengthen our working relationships but also help create a culture where respect and collaboration flourish.

Reflection

- ❖ One way I can lighten my supervisor's load this week is:

  _____

- ❖ A consistent habit I can build to strengthen our team culture is:

  _____

NOTES

ABOUT THE AUTHOR

Beverly K. Girton is the founder and principal consultant of *Leading the LIGHT Way HR, LLC.* With more than two decades of experience in human resources and leadership development, she has devoted her life to equipping leaders to walk in Love, Integrity, Goodness, Humility, and Transparency.

Beverly holds an MBA in Management and Conflict Resolution from Dallas Baptist University. She is also a certified mediator and an experienced trainer, drawing on both professional expertise and spiritual wisdom to help leaders serve well and avoid burnout.

She is passionate about reducing church hurt, strengthening unity, and helping leaders "light the path and lighten the load."

www.ingramcontent.com/pod-product-compliance
Lightning Source LLC
Chambersburg PA
CBHW051541120626
46551CB00013B/1324